Our Travel Bucket List

Imagine, create and plan the destinations of your life together.

Anita Kaltenbaugh

∞

Destination Escape Press
Somewhere in the desert, sea and forest.
∞
Destination Escape supports copyright for all authors.
Thank you for purchasing a copyrighted edition of this book.
First Edition 2018

ISBN- 978-1986875875

Travel, the one thing you buy
that makes your richer
-unknown

Let's get rich!

This book belongs to:

It is OUR travel bucket list.

We can go wherever we want to go. We will explore this world together. These are our dream destinations.

We started our bucket list on this date:

_____

I don't want to be
"tied down" to
someone, I want to
be "set free" with
someone.
-unknown

Scribble, write, erase, draw, doodle, or write love notes to each other. Write important dates down, journal, write a song, write a poem, write words. This is your space together. Someday you'll be glad you kept this notebook and you'll treasure your dreams.

Introduction:

This book is for YOUR journey as a couple.

The places the two of you will explore in your lifetime.

Where do you want to go? What do you want to see?

The world is yours to traverse, the planet spins as do your ideas together, and there are so many choices of places to stop and get off.

Allow me to be the first to congratulate you both.

Congratulations. Congratulations on being together and planning together.

As a couple you are way ahead of most of the world. You're creating a Travel Bucket List. Dreaming on paper, making the words you write down, a possible reality. Sharing ideas and fantasy locations can only add to your enriched life.

Writing things down with pen or pencil, will help both of you see your dreams and inspirations clearly in life. Yes, I believe there is something empowering about looking at words, words that only existed in your thoughts, in printed or cursive form. Better yet, thoughts you took the time to share with each other.

I always loved the quote, "If you don't know where you are going, how will you know when you get there?" It's true, we often need a road map of where we are headed, and yet sometimes, it's the journey getting to our designated point that ends up changing our lives. Sometimes it's sharing these ideas with each other.

It doesn't matter when you begin your Travel Bucket List. Maybe you just met, or you have been together forever. Maybe you are engaged or have pledged your life to each other.

Honeymoon? A perfect place to take a few moments out of every new day together, to explore your future travel plans and destinations.
It doesn't matter when you start this adventure, it only matters that you began this journey together.

Where do you want to go? What do you want to see?
Some folks desire to see every state in
the United States, or every country in Europe,
South America, Africa, or Asia. Some might have a list of
local places they have never taken the time or
energy to see.

There are no wrong answers.

It is about what you both want to see and sharing your ideas.

My travel bucket list consisted of a stop at every continent. Luckily, my partner agreed with me. But, he didn't know that until we took the time to talk about it.

You may have very different top ten lists, and that is great. How magnificent to explore each other's hope and dreams together. On each of the following pages, record both your answers. Write all the ideas you share and don't share.

In this book, there are no rules. You can create your travel bucket list, add to it, or delete from it. You are in charge and you can change it as many times as you like.

So where do you want to go?

There are either 7 or 8 total continents on this planet and 195 countries depending on which school of thought you subscribe to. United Nations has 193 countries as members and 2 observer states, so I'll go with 195.

I'm going with the 7 continents of the world as: **North America, South America, Antarctica, Europe, Asia, Africa and Australia.**

As of right now, I have three continents to go to fulfill my goal of touching every continent but loads of countries to visit. I've been fortunate to travel often, and a few years ago I logged over 99 vacations in three years. I even wrote a book about how I was able to plan and afford my journey. *Travel Secrets: An Insider guide to planning, affording and taking more vacations.* So be sure to check the book out to learn how to afford your list. It's free on Kindle Unlimited.

But, the purpose of this book is to make your lists. Where do you want to go? Where do you want to go together?

So, where do you want to go?

This is a journal to figure out what destinations **you** most desire to explore. Where does your heart or your mind escape to when you have that moment of peace? What have you been longing to see up close? Maybe it's around the corner, or far away. There are no right answers.
It's a big world out there and the list of possibilities of places to explore are endless.

Keep a log of your travels. Trust me you think you will remember but you won't.

Write down how many vacations you take in a year, a decade, and in your life. Share them with your family or friends.

Leave this journal for your parents, children, best friend or closest companions.

Or, perhaps just keep it for yourself, with a cord tied around it, and see how many bucket items you can achieve. (For some other fantastic journals go to www.bookswithsoul.com.)

Check the boxes.
Cross out the names and places you visited, write the date you traveled beside the names on your list.

Write in it, draw in it, doodle, scribble, do what you wish.

Paste photos of places you long to go. Pictures you ripped out of a magazine. Carry it in the rain, bend the pages, rip a few out—just do what you want.

It doesn't matter, there are no rules. It is your Travel Bucket List.

And, don't forget, if you need some help on ways to afford more trips, Check out, *Travel Secrets: An Insider guide to planning, affording and taking more vacations,* available on Amazon and Barnes and Noble, as an eBook or print.

You can use this journal as a companion
or use it independently. Whatever you do,
create your Travel Bucket List, and take
more vacations together.

We live in a remarkable era of technology –
    and because of this travel has never been easier,
    more accessible or more affordable.

We only have ourselves to blame for not planning
    more time-off to visit the destinations that are
    alive in our mind. And, not knowing the destinations
    that exist in your other half's mind.

Take the time in your life to figure out your
            Travel Bucket List,
    and then get busy making it happen.

    If you dream it, it can happen.

    EXPL ORE and take notes, so you can have a
    written history of your adventures.

Adventure Awaits.

The first step of a living your travel dreams,
is knowing where and what they are.
Create a road map and set goals.

If you want to travel more, you can.
The first step is figuring out where.

This is a place for your dreams,
your travel bucket list together,
by writing it down,
you are on the road to achieving it.

"The world is a book and those who do not travel read only one page." – St.

Augustine

OUR
TOP 5 PLACES
TO SEE

THE FIRST 5 LOCATIONS THAT POP IN MY MIND
THEY CAN BE ANYWHERE ON THIS PLANET

Is it more difficult than you imagined creating a top 5 list together?

Okay, now try to complete your own list (turn the page) and see what happens...

LET'S THINK ABOUT

MY
TOP 5 PLACES
TO SEE

THE FIRST 5 LOCATIONS THAT POP IN MY MIND
THEY CAN BE ANYWHERE ON THIS PLANET

LET'S THINK ABOUT

MY
TOP 5 PLACES
TO SEE

THE FIRST 5 LOCATIONS THAT POP IN MY MIND
THEY CAN BE ANYWHERE ON THIS PLANET

LET'S THINK ABOUT

PLACES WE DREAM OF

THE FIRST TEN PLACES THAT POP IN MY MIND

Again, if you need some help, try completing your own list individually (on the following pages) and compare, see what you have in common, where you differ.

Continue the next several pages, answering the questions together.

List the continents you have traveled to together, and the ones you have been to on you own. Record both your answers.

LET'S THINK ABOUT

PLACES I DREAM OF

THE FIRST TEN PLACES THAT POP IN MY MIND

LET'S THINK ABOUT

PLACES I DREAM OF

THE FIRST TEN PLACES THAT POP IN MY MIND

List of the 7 continents:

North America:

South America:

Europe:

Asia:

Australia:

Antartica:

Africa:

LET'S THINK ABOUT :

PLACES I WANT TO SEE IN THE USA

LET'S THINK ABOUT :

PLACES I WANT TO SEE IN AFRICA

LET'S THINK ABOUT :

PLACES I WANT TO SEE IN CENTRAL AMERICA

LET'S THINK ABOUT :

PLACES I WANT TO SEE IN NORTH AMERICA

LET'S THINK ABOUT :

PLACES I WANT TO SEE IN EUROPE

LET'S THINK ABOUT :

PLACES I WANT TO SEE IN ANTARTICA

LET'S THINK ABOUT :

PLACES I WANT TO SEE IN AUSTRALIA,/NEW ZEALAND/NEW CALEDONIA

LET'S THINK ABOUT :

PLACES I WANT TO SEE IN ASIA

LET'S THINK ABOUT :

PLACES I WANT TO SEE IN A DAY'S DRIVE

LET'S THINK ABOUT :

PLACES I WANT TO SEE IN MY 50 MILE RADIUS

LET'S THINK ABOUT

FAVORITE VACATIONS

WHY DID I LOVE THEM?

OUR TRAVEL BUCKET LIST

DATE :
TOP 10 PLACES WE WANT TO SEE

Use this list,

"Our Travel Bucket List" as a place to start.

Change it as many times as you want.

Go through the rest of the journal. Write your thoughts, ideas, scribble, doodle, and answer a few of the questions, or read the quotes. Discuss places, dream destinations, and off the beaten hidden gems. Show each other exciting images online. Scratch down new locations. Brainstorm.

At the back of the book is another blank travel bucket list. You can write your new travel bucket list there, after you have worked your way through the pages.

"To live is the rarest thing in the world. Most people exist, that is all." Oscar Wilde

Life is too short, make your list, and get busy living.

Sometimes, I want to escape all the stress and go here:

Take the Travel Quiz and compare
with your partner:

Do you think you like the same type of
vacations?
Answer the questions individually,
then compare answers. Understand
what your partner likes.
This exercise will help you start to
make a bucket list you both enjoy.

Quiz: What kind of traveler are you?
Take the following quiz. Read the questions out loud and answer the questions as an individual. Score to find out what kind of traveler you are. Compare answers as a couple.

1. In my mind, the word vacation conjures up an image that fits in one of these categories:
   a. Beach scene, island, tropical
   b. Skyscrapers, vibrant city scene, fantastic food
   c. Woods, forest, trails, trees
   d. Landmarks, old castles, museums, history
2. If I had to choose one of the following activities to do on my vacation, I would choose:
   a. A lounge chair, blue water, a good book, a frozen cocktail
   b. Sightseeing, trains, night clubs, shopping
   c. Hiking, skiing, camping, biking
   d. Tours to little known places, art, history, knowledge
3. You scored a free vacation, which one would you pick?
   a. All-inclusive resort vacation in Turks and Caicos
   b. 4 nights in Manhattan, with show tickets
   c. An RV for a week in Colorado
   d. A European guided tour of castles.
4. Which type of movie/series do you most want to watch?
   a. Bay Watch, Fools Gold, Secret islands of the world. or Cocktail
   b. Sex and the City, Man on the Ledge, Foodie City Style
   c. Into the Wild, The Edge, The Great Outdoors, Everest
   d. Downton Abbey, The Da Vinci Code, The History channel
5. Pick a song out of the following you would like to hear right now:
   a. No Shoes No Shirt No problem
   b. New York New York
   c. Take me Home Country Road
   d. Brahms Symphony No 1

6. What do you most feel like packing on a trip?
    a. Bathing suits, shorts, t-shirts, flip flops, beachy dresses
    b. Fly clothes, club clothes, clothes that make a statement
    c. hiking boots, shorts, hats, jeans, outdoor wear
    d. Comfortable clothes, walking shoes, things that pack well
7. Pick a food that sounds good to you in this moment:
    a. Shrimp, fish, fresh fruit, tropical salads, lobster
    b. Tapas, foie gras, steak, eclectic dishes, sashimi
    c. Hamburgers, hotdogs, grilled steaks, barbeque
    d. Local dishes, chocolate, Indian food, German schnitzel
8. Pick a drink you would like to order:
    a. Margarita, frozen cocktail, island local beer
    b. Cosmopolitan, champagne, Harvey wall banger,
    c. Beer, vodka, wine
    d. Pilsner, tea, coffee, port
9. Would you rather?
    a. Sit on a lounge chair listening to the waves
    b. Read your newspaper in the middle of a city outdoor café
    c. Stretch out on a blanket in the middle of the woods
    d. Eat lunch at a café in the middle of an Art Museum

Count 1 for every a, b, c, d, you have:

A= _____

B= _____

C= _____

D= _____

Answers:

A- If you have 6-9 A's, Hello beach lover. Islands, tropical weather & toes in the sand sounds like a great vacation to you. Pick an island you have never stepped foot on and go!

B- If you have 6-9 B's, you thrive in the city. People watching, night life and the energy of the crowds wake you up. Check out a city center you have never visited and immerse yourself in the city.

C- If you scored 6-9 C's, you are a back to nature kind of person. Explore the off the beaten track places. Hike to somewhere most people never see in their lifetime.

D- If you scored 6-9 D's, you love history. You seek out places that tell a story, locations that shed light on where we came from. Check out a medieval city, or a city in the national historic registry.

3-5 A's, you like the beach, it's on your list, but you like to mix it up with a variety of vacations.

3-5 B's, you enjoy the city. but you like variety & change

3-5 C's, you love nature and off the beaten track but not all the time.

3-5 D's, History is fascinating to you, and you want to explore a slice of it on your vacation.

1-2 A's, the beach is not your first choice, but you will try a tropical vacation if your other half wants to.

1-2 B's, the city is okay for some things.

1-2 C's. You can visit nature but not please no camping.

1-2 D's, you enjoy a little history, maybe 1 museum every 2 years.

Zero A's, don't go to the beach.

Zero B's, stay away from the city for vacations.

Zero C's, stay out of the woods.

Zero D's, take a nap while your partner goes to a museum.

Run away together...

"Life is either a daring adventure or nothing." -- Helen Keller

Do you know how many countries there are in the world?

There are 193 or 195 countries in the world, depending on how you look at it.

List of all the countries in the world:

A

- Afghanistan
- Albania
- Algeria
- Andorra
- Angola
- Antigua and Barbuda
- Argentina
- Armenia
- Aruba
- Australia
- Austria
- Azerbaijan

B

- Bahamas, The
- Bahrain
- Bangladesh
- Barbados
- Belarus
- Belgium
- Belize
- Benin
- Bhutan
- Bolivia
- Bosnia and Herzegovina
- Botswana
- Brazil
- Brunei
- Bulgaria
- Burkina Faso
- Burma
- Burundi

C

- Cambodia
- Cameroon
- Canada
- Cabo Verde
- Central African Republic
- Chad
- Chile
- China
- Colombia
- Comoros
- Congo, Democratic Republic of the
- Congo, Republic of the
- Costa Rica
- Cote d'Ivoire
- Croatia
- Cuba
- Curacao
- Cyprus
- Czechia

D

- Denmark
- Djibouti
- Dominica
- Dominican Republic

E

- East Timor (see Timor-Leste)
- Ecuador
- Egypt
- El Salvador
- Equatorial Guinea
- Eritrea
- Estonia
- Ethiopia

F

- Fiji
- Finland
- France

G

- Gabon
- Gambia, The
- Georgia
- Germany
- Ghana
- Greece
- Grenada
- Guatemala
- Guinea
- Guinea-Bissau
- Guyana

H

- Haiti
- Holy See
- Honduras
- Hong Kong
- Hungary

I

- Iceland
- India
- Indonesia
- Iran
- Iraq
- Ireland
- Israel
- Italy

J

- Jamaica
- Japan
- Jordan

K

- Kazakhstan
- Kenya
- Kiribati
- Korea, North
- Korea, South
- Kosovo
- Kuwait
- Kyrgyzstan

L

- Laos
- Latvia
- Lebanon
- Lesotho
- Liberia
- Libya
- Liechtenstein
- Lithuania
- Luxembourg

M

- Macau
- Macedonia
- Madagascar
- Malawi
- Malaysia
- Maldives
- Mali
- Malta
- Marshall Islands
- Mauritania
- Mauritius
- Mexico
- Micronesia
- Moldova
- Monaco
- Mongolia
- Montenegro
- Morocco
- Mozambique

N

- Namibia
- Nauru
- Nepal
- Netherlands
- New Zealand
- Nicaragua
- Niger
- Nigeria
- North Korea
- Norway

O

- Oman

P

- Pakistan
- Palau
- Palestinian Territories
- Panama
- Papua New Guinea
- Paraguay
- Peru
- Philippines
- Poland
- Portugal

Q

- Qatar

R

- Romania
- Russia
- Rwanda

S

- Saint Kitts and Nevis
- Saint Lucia
- Saint Vincent and the Grenadines
- Samoa
- San Marino

- Sao Tome and Principe
- Saudi Arabia
- Senegal
- Serbia
- Seychelles
- Sierra Leone
- Singapore
- Sint Maarten
- Slovakia
- Slovenia
- Solomon Islands
- Somalia
- South Africa
- South Korea
- South Sudan
- Spain
- Sri Lanka
- Sudan
- Suriname
- Swaziland
- Sweden
- Switzerland
- Syria

T

- Taiwan
- Tajikistan
- Tanzania
- Thailand
- Timor-Leste
- Togo
- Tonga
- Trinidad and Tobago
- Tunisia
- Turkey
- Turkmenistan
- Tuvalu

U

- Uganda
- Ukraine
- United Arab Emirates
- United Kingdom
- Uruguay
- Uzbekistan

V

- Vanuatu
- Venezuela
- Vietnam

Y

- Yemen

Z

- Zambia
- Zimbabwe

Circle the countries you want to see.
Look up ones you never heard of.
Explore.

The list of countries can differ from different sources. This list is from:

The U.S. Department of State.

https://www.state.gov/misc/list/index.htm

Remember when you travel, to take time to pause, and live in the moment of where you are.

Live in the sunshine, swim in the sea, drink the wild air- Ralph Waldo Emerson

Name a few off the beaten places you would love to explore:

"Do one thing every day
that
scares you."
-- Eleanor Roosevelt

Write down what scares you about
traveling.

I see a photo of this destination and I can't stop thinking about it:

I picture us here someday.

I haven't been everywhere, but
I'm making a list.

Sometimes, I want to escape all the stress and go here:

Where to next?

Tired of hotel rooms? Want a home away from home?
Try Airbnb.
AirBNB is my favorite way to travel. I get more than just a bed and bathroom.
Experience how it feels to live like a local. I have stayed in an oceanfront condo in the Dominican Republic, a beach house in Santa Cruz, CA, a loft in Knoxville, TN and many more. Every rental has been awesome.

If you have never used AirBNB, use this code on a first time reservation and receive $40 off. (Airbnb can change this offer at any time and is only for first time users of Airbnb.)

For $40 off first reservation. Paste this link or click on this link and sign up: www.airbnb.com/c/anitak103

Do you know where you're going?

You both win a free airline ticket...
 But to use it, you must pick a destination, and shout the location out loud, in one minute.
(anywhere in the world) What destination would you shout?

Try this one together, time yourself and in 60 seconds shout your destination.

"Though we travel the world over to find the beautiful, we must carry it with us, or we find it not." Ralph Waldo Emerson

If I only knew that magical place--that magical spot that makes me feel at home, and yet I have never been there?

You can never cross the ocean until you

have the courage to lose sight

of the shore. Christopher Columbus

Bid on a travel auction. It might be the destination you didn't even know you were supposed to see together.

∞ infinite possibilities

Die with memories not dreams -unknown

"Keep your face to the sunshine and you can never see the shadow."

- *Helen Keller*

"In life, it's not where you go, it's who you travel with"
-Charles Schulz

Let's hold hands and see the world.

LET'S THINK ABOUT

PLACES I DREAM OF

THE FIRST TEN PLACES THAT POP IN MY MIND

Sometimes we just need to say "Yes" more often.

Where do you want to say yes to?

The whole secret of a successful life is to find out what is one's destiny to do, and then do it." — Henry Ford

"You only live once, but if you do it right, once is enough." -- *Mae West*

Travel far enough, and you may find out who you really are. A.K. Smith

"It does not matter how slowly you go, so long as you do not stop."
- *Confucius*

Traveling it leaves you speechless, then turns you into a storyteller.
IBN BATTUTA

"Learn from yesterday, live for today, hope for tomorrow. The important thing is not to stop questioning." -- *Albert Einstein*

Go see the world the way you want.

If you want to see it together, wherever it is located, you can.

Make a
PLAN

Fill your life with adventures not things. Have stories to tell not to stuff to show.

Looking at the ocean can cure all my worries

Will you follow your dreams?

Only put off until tomorrow what you are
willing to die having left undone."
-*Pablo Picasso*

Write your top 2 travel destinations
on a piece
of paper.
include your email address and your
names,
Write, "This is where we want to
Travel to..."
Roll it up, place it in a bottle
and ...wait for it...don't toss it out to sea.
It will probably end up in a floating
garbage dump.

So, instead ...hide it somewhere you
might find it in the future, or where
someone else might discover it.

Who knows...when you see it years later,
maybe your travel dreams came true.

. "Happiness is a butterfly, which when pursued, is always beyond your grasp, but which, if you will sit down quietly, may alight upon you." -- *Nathaniel Hawthorne*

As soon as I saw you, I knew our life together would be an adventure we would never forget.

Anita Kaltenbaugh

Why not go?

Travel far enough outside of who you think you are and you might meet your true self. A.K. Smith

Traveling it leaves you speechless, then turns you into a storyteller.
IBN BATTUTA

Traveling makes one **modest,** you see the tiny space **you occupy** in the **world.** -Gustave Flaubert

The world is big and I want to get a good look at it before it gets dark. - John Muir

Just do it.

Just go.

Better to see something once than
hear about it a thousand times.
-Asian Proverb

Make a list of the countries you have visited.

List the names of the countries you visited:

List the country you most want to see before you die.

Life teaches us many things,
but travel with
someone you love and
you'll know if you're meant
to be together...

"He who does not travel does not know the value of men."– Moorish proverb

I watched a movie,
and
now I want to go here:

I heard a song, and now I want to go here:

You won a sweepstakes.

Now you need to pick a

destination...?

If I won an all-expense-paid vacation, I would go to:

If we were meant to stay in one place, we'd have roots instead of feet. - anon

Pick a letter in the alphabet, any letter. Look at the list of 195 countries under that letter, now pick one, research it together and go!

It is never too late to be what you might have been. - George Eliot

Adventure is worthwhile- Aesop

One of my favorite books takes place here:

Plan your vacations
and they will happen.

One of the best Vacations Ever:

Sometimes the best anniversary present is taking a trip together.

For my part, I travel not to go anywhere, but to go, I travel for travel's sake. The great affair is to move. -Robert Louis Stevenson

We travel not to escape
life, but for life to escape us

-unknown

An empty beach, a setting sun, now I can relax in perfect solitude. A.K. Smith

If I want to go somewhere, see a specific destination...then I need to figure out a way to make it happen.

See the world, maybe even the moon.

I dream of this place:

And we will travel
    together
And just be in love
    Forever -unknown

Actually, the best gift you could have given her was a lifetime of adventures...Lewis Carroll Alice in Wonderland

Go find your Alice

Let's travel this world together.

If you need an escape, go somewhere together off the beaten path.

They say there's a place at the end of the rainbow filled with gold…go forth and find your end of the rainbow…wherever it is, you'll find riches better than gold. A.K. Smith

I always wanted to see the _____.

Take me:

If we can imagine a place of beauty and peace than we must find it...

If I close my eyes I picture myself here:

To move, to breathe, to fly, to float, to roam the roads of lands remote, to travel is to live.

Hans Christian Andersen

Always take the scenic route

We need to save money to go here:

And so the adventure begins

Let's start a savings account for our travel bucket list.

Are you ready?

Log of our travels:

Date/Place

Date/Place

Date/Place

Date/Place

Date/Place

Date/Place

Date/Place

Date/Place

Date/Place

Date/Place

Date/Place

Date/Place

Date/Place

Date/Place

Date/Place

Date/Place

Date/Place

Date/Place

Date/Place

Date/Place

Date/Place

Date/Place

Date/Place

Date/Place

Date/Place

Date/Place

Date/Place

Date/Place

Date/Place

Date/Place

Date/Place

Date/Place

Date/Place

Date/Place

Date/Place

Date/Place

Date/Place

Date/Place

Date/Place

Date/Place

Date/Place

Date/Place

Date/Place

Date/Place

Date/Place

Date/Place

Date/Place

Date/Place

Date/Place

Date/Place

Date/Place

Date/Place

Date/Place

Date/Place

Date/Place

Date/Place

Date/Place

_____

Date/Place

_____

Date/Place

_____

Date/Place

_____

I hope you take so many vacations, you need
more pages. Fill them up, mark down every time
you get away, even if it's a night away.
Record your memories and experiences while
traveling and you will never forget.

Take vacations, your life and your partner will thank you for it. See the world, and become alive, stop thinking about it and do it.

"Be yourself. Everyone else is already taken." -- *Oscar Wilde*

Are you seeing your travel bucket list start to grow?

Start with writing down a top ten list for the two of you and start crossing off the list as you make incredible memories.

MY TRAVEL BUCKET LIST

DATE :
TOP 10 PLACES I WANT TO SEE

1
2
3
4
5
6
7
8
9
10

Remember,
this is your
life,
See what you
want to
See.
Go where you
want to go.
Make a plan,
And it will
Happen.

Are you ready?

GET YOUR COPY OF INSIDER SECRETS

Check out Travel Secrets: Insider guide to planning, affording and taking more vacations on Amazon. Free on Kindle Unlimited.

A guide to help you achieve your bucket list.

I would like to travel the world with you twice. Once to see the world. Twice, to see the way you see the world. – Anon

Our top 10 travel bucket list:

(A list to start our travels together):

1.

2.

3.

4.

5.

6.

7.

8.

9.

10.

Who knows what will
happen to our data
in the future?

Celebrate the art of writing
by choosing to pen your words
on paper.

Check out Books With Soul
Bookswithsoul.com
Your Words. Your Pages.